101

Things to Do In

DOOR

COUNTY

Copyright 2004
Richard R. Rusnack II

D0094223

~101 Things To Do In Door County~

Copyright 2004
Richard R. Rusnack II

ISBN 0-9759604-0-7
First Edition – 1996
Revised Edition – 1996, 2000, 2004

Published by Rusnack Publishing
Ellison Bay, WI 54210

Manufactured in the United States of America

Introduction

This little collection of ideas began as a simple itinerary I created for a guest who asked me to map out a full weekend of things to do in Door County. It seemed like such a perfect way to keep my guests happy and busy during their visits that I started a little journal of ideas, and continued adding to it for years. That tattered list, which started as just a few reminders, has somehow made it onto the pages of this little book.

This is a very personal listing of suggestions I have shared over the years with family and friends. Some businesses are mentioned but this is not meant to be an advertisement, these are places which have stoood the test of time and have long been family favorites.

I hope you will use this book in much the same way I have; consider it a puzzle that can be assembled a thousand different ways; choose at random and build a day, a week, a summer, just use your imagination and the key to the Door is yours.

"ILLE TERRARUM MIHI PRAETER
OMNIS ANGULUS RIDET"
~Horace Odes 2, 6, 13-14

<u>*Translation*</u> *:*
This little corner of the earth
to me smiles
beyond all others.

~101 Things To Do In Door County~

Dedicated to the memory of my Father,
Richard Rusnack,
I will always feel your hand at the helm;
and to
Rachel, Hannah, & Griffin,
the loves of my life.

Highway 57

• 1 •

Applaud a sunset
from Ellison Bay Bluff Park.

It is the best performance in the county. Take Hwy. 42 three miles north of Sister Bay, turn left on Porcupine Road, travel west about one half mile, then turn right at the (small) brown park sign onto a gravel road. The road will lead into the woods for about a mile and then slowly bend to the left, finally delivering you to the most spectacular view in Door County.

• 2 •

Walk the Fern Trail at Newport State Park.

One of the most beautiful places in Door County is a small section of the Fern Trail in Newport State Park. Follow Hwy 42 north past Ellison Bay and then follow County NP to the third parking lot. Start your hike by following the Europe Bay Trail to the north, and then turn left onto the Fern Trail. About 1/3 mile onto Fern the woods open up to a sea of ferns. Stop for a few minutes just to enjoy the view. Make sure to stay on the trail and leave the fragile area undisturbed. You will definitely want to come back to this little known slice of heaven.

• 3 •

Visit the monument in Ephraim, which commemorates the landing of the Moravians in 1853.

The Moravian's landing site also happens to be the place where French explorer Jean Nicolet came ashore wearing oriental robes believing he had discovered a water-passage to Asia. After spending a few days with the Winnebago Indians, the great explorer took off the robes. While you contemplate Ephraim's history, grab an ice cream cone from Wilson's – a Door County institution.

• 4 •

Discover one of the last great small-town talent shows.

On the Friday night before the Olde Ellison Bay Days Festival begins (last weekend in June). The fire trucks pull out of the firehouse for the night to provide an improvised theatre, and the show begins. The evening is a delightful parade of musicians, singers, dancers, and storytellers.

• 5 •

Find the original cabin of Asa Thorpe, one of Door County's earliest settlers, and Founder of Fish Creek.

The old log home is behind the shops at Founder's square on Main Street in Fish Creek. Grab a little sustenance at the Door County Confectionery, and then follow the wood-chip path to the right of their front door and you will be led to Asa's old homestead. (Imagine raising your family in a house the size of your bedroom.)

Ephraim

• 6 •

Stroll into the past; visit the Ephraim Foundation Museums.

See the Anderson Store, Anderson Barn, Pioneer Schoolhouse and Goodletson Cabin just off Hwy 42 along the north rim of Eagle Harbor in Ephraim. You can visit the museums on your own, but we recommend the walking tour offered Monday, Wednesday and Friday, mid-June through early September.

www.ephraim.org
Email: efoundation@itol.com

• 7 •

Tap your toes to a concert at the Birch Creek Barn.

From the road, it looks like just another barn, but do not be fooled. This barn is home to the Birch Creek Music Performance Center. Operating by day as a performance camp for some of our most promising young musicians, the 500-seat barn transforms at sunset into one of the county's most unique settings. Throughout the summer, the sounds change from Symphony to Percussion to Big Band.

www.birchcreek.org

(920) 868-3763

• 8 •

Hike to a theatre in the woods.

Another classic is the American Folklore Theater located under the stars in Peninsula State Park. Our favorite way to enjoy the show is to make it the grand finale of a family day in the park. Pack a picnic and drive to the Nicolet Beach parking lot. Before you unpack the car, grab a trail map and follow the Nicolet Bay trail. It is about a 2.2-mile loop that will bring you back to the beach for a day of swimming and picnicking. Bring a change of clothes and plenty of bug spray for the show that begins at dusk.

www.folkloretheatre.com
(920) 854-6117

• 9 •

Plan a day to explore your artsy side.

The Peninsula Art School has workshops for all ages and abilities, and even welcomes the artistically impaired. With so many ways to express yourself, painting, drawing, pottery, jewelry, photography and more; you cannot help but discover a few hidden talents.

www.peninsulaartschool.com
(920) 868-3455

• 10 •

Scuba dive the shipwrecks of Death's Door.

If you are willing to be a little more adventurous, plan a day of scuba diving. Much of Door County's early mystique developed around tales of its treacherous waters. Dozens of shipwrecks fill the coastal waters, and there are stories of one or two ghostly wrecks that sit upright on the bottom, masts still aloft and fully rigged. Dinosaur Divers located at the Shoreline Resort in Gills Rock can take you to many of these sites.

(920) 854-2606

Lake Michigan Shore

• 11 •

Try to golf all 27 holes at the Alpine Golf Course.

This is one of Door County's original golf course resorts and remains one of its most popular. There is a breathtaking view of the bay from the blufftop hole number 9, and a tram to take you there. After this much golf reward yourself with dinner at *the hof*, the resort's waterfront restaurant.

www.alpineresort.com
(920) 868-3232

• 12 •

Do you know a great place for …?

As Door County retailers, the question we are asked more than any other is, "where should we eat?" In fact, many ideas for this book came from a section of our store's newsletter titled, "Tried and True." This was where we listed our favorite places to dine and stay, according to our own personal opinions. On the next few pages, you will find our current picks.

• 13 •

Tried and True
for Breakfast:

White Gull Inn	Fish Creek
The Cookery	Fish Creek
Viking Grill	Ellison Bay
Village Café	Egg Harbor
Sister Bay Café	Sister Bay
Al Johnson's	Sister Bay
Old Post Office	Ephraim
Good Eggs	Ephraim
Bluefront Café	Sturgeon Bay

• 14 •

Tried and True
for Lunch:

Inn at Cedar Crossing	Sturgeon Bay
PC Junction	Peninsula Center
Coyote Roadhouse	Bailey's Harbor
Diggers	Fish Creek
Fish Creek General Store	Fish Creek
Hitching Post	Valmy
D'Amico's	Sister Bay
drink coffee	Sister Bay
Fred & Fuzzy's	Sister Bay

• 15 •
Tried and True
for Dinner:

Glidden Lodge	Sturgeon Bay
Sage	Sturgeon Bay
Mr. Helsinki	Fish Creek
Inn at Kristoffer's	Sister Bay
Alexander's	Sister Bay
Greenwood	Fish Creek
J.J.'s La Puerta	Sister Bay
Whistling Swan	Fish Creek
Shoreline	Gills Rock
T. Ashwell's	Ellison Bay
English Inn	Fish Creek
Northern Grill	Sister Bay
Sister Bay Bowl	Sister Bay

• 16 •

Tried and True
Night Life:

AC Tap	Bailey's Harbor
Husby's	Sister Bay
Blue Ox	Bailey's Harbor
Peninsula Pub	Peninsula Center
Casey's	Egg Harbor
Van's	Sturgeon Bay
Bayside Tavern	Fish Creek
Mink River Basin	Ellison Bay
Nelsen's Hall Bitters Pub	Washington Island

• 17 •

Tried and True Lodging:

White Gull Inn	Fish Creek
Homestead Suites	Fish Creek
Blacksmith Inn	Bailey's Harbor
Hotel Disgarden	Ellison Bay
Grand View	Ellison Bay
Hillside Inn	Ephraim
Juniper Inn	Ephraim
Eagle Harbor Inn	Ephraim
Inn on Maple	Sister Bay
Wooden Heart	Sister Bay
Scandia Lodge	Sister Bay
Church Hill Inn	Sister Bay
Glidden Lodge	Sturgeon Bay
The Scofield House	Sturgeon Bay
Reynolds House	Sturgeon Bay
Stone Harbor	Sturgeon Bay
White Lace Inn	Sturgeon Bay

Peninsula State Park

• 18 •
Take a Sunday stroll down Cottage Row.

Our favorite Sunday morning starts with breakfast at the White Gull Inn on Main St. in Fish Creek. Splurge on a slice of their famous Door County-berry sour cream coffee cake; then take a much needed stroll down Cottage Row. From The White Gull Inn follow Main St. to Cottage Row and turn right. The walk will take you north along the row of shoreline "cottages" about 1 mile before it turns up the steep bluff. At the base of the bluff is a sliver of a park known as Champagne Rock, named for the little rock that hangs over the water. Down and back is a perfect way to walk off breakfast and start the day.

• 19 •

See the flames fly at a Scandinavian Fish Boil.

Door County is famous for fish boils. The traditional meal of whitefish, red potatoes, and cherry pie is served in many forms all over the county. The whitefish and potatoes are boiled together in a large black kettle, after the fish is fully cooked; the boil master throws kerosene on the fire to boil off the oils that have risen to the surface during cooking. The flames can reach 20 feet into the air, and offer a spectacular grand finale to the show – then it is time for dinner. Our favorite is the experience at the White Gull Inn. During peak season, you may need to reserve a few days in advance.

(920) 868-3517

• 20 •

Discover a secret paradise-
Europe Lake.

The water is warm, the crowd is small and I guarantee it will be one of your new favorite spots. Pack a picnic and a kayak, canoe, or inner tube; then just let the day slip by on Door County time. To get to one of the few public access points, follow Hwy 42 north to Europe Bay Road, turn left on Timberline Road, and then right onto Europe Lake Road. The entire eastern border of the lake is Newport State park, so paddle your way across, then beach your craft and go for a hike!

• 21 •

The theatre is the star of the show at Peninsula Players.

This waterfront, open-air theatre provides the setting for a perfect night out. Our favorite way to enjoy the theatre is to arrive about an hour early, so we can enjoy the sunset over a bottle of wine and a picnic before the curtain call. You will find one of the best wine selections in Door County and a wonderful gourmet deli at the Main Street Market in Egg Harbor. To get to Peninsula Players, follow Hwy 42 to Peninsula Players Road, and then turn west. Be sure to reserve your tickets in advance.

(920) 868 – 3287

• 22 •

Weather the storm at Cave Point.

Go to Cave Point on a stormy day to watch the waves crash against the bluffs. The park access road is just south of Jacksonport on Hwy 57. For a beautiful drive on the way to the park, follow N. Cave Point Drive from Jacksonport through the woods and along Lake Michigan until you arrive at Cave Point County Park.

Fish Creek Harbor

• 23 •

Door County's best waterfront dining.

Pick up a couple of sandwiches from the deli at the back of the Fish Creek General Store. Grab your lunch and walk down toward the harbor on Spruce Street, turn right on Maple Street, then walk all of the way out to the end of the Fish Creek Municipal Dock. Have a seat on one of the benches and enjoy one of the best lunch spots in the world!

• 24 •

Do you have what it takes to join the Polar Bear Club?

The annual meeting convened at the Jacksonport Park in January. Initiation is simple: just run into the frozen lake like a crazy person while screaming at the top of your lungs; if you do not have a heart attack – you are in!

• 25 •

Get a taste of Napa Valley at Door County's wineries.

Designate a driver and plan a day of tasting at our favorite Door County wineries:

Lautenbach's Orchard Country Winery (Fish Creek)
Door Peninsula Winery (Carlsville)
Stone's Throw (Peninsula Center)
Simon Creek (Jacksonport)

Horseshoe Island

• 26 •

*Rent a Jet Ski in Ephraim
and thrash the waves of
Eagle Harbor.*

• 27 •

Go for a hike!

Door county's State Parks can look crowded during the summer months until you realize that few people ever leave their cars. Even if the parking lot looks full, I guarantee plenty of solitude at the far end of the trail. Here is one of our favorite hikes: park your car at Cave Point County Park and follow the white trail to the north of the lot. This 2.5 mile trail will take you past Cave Point, and then into the woods for just the right distance before looping back to your car.

• 28 •

The standards are low, but spirits are high at the Fish Creek Winter Games, February.

(920) 868 - 2316

• 29 •

Sail away from it all
on Eagle Harbor.

Rent a sailboat in Ephraim from the town dock, and then sail across Eagle Harbor and into Nicolet Bay. This is Peninsula State Park's heart of waterfront activity. You can beach your boat and grab lunch or an ice cream in the beachfront snack bar.

Sailing on Eagle Harbor

• 30 •

All-aboooard!
Here comes lunch on
a flatbed train.

The kids are going to love this one! The whistle blows, the wheels turn, and the conductor bellows, "Fish Creek, next stop" as your lunch chugs toward you on the flatbed car of a toy train! P.C. Junction, at the corner of County Roads A and E, due east of Egg Harbor is a true Door County original.

• 31 •

Get lost in the reeds of Kangaroo Lake's north end.

Take a guided kayak tour of Kangaroo Lake's north end; only reachable by boat, it remains one of Door County's most pristine and secluded wilderness areas. We recommend Bayshore Outdoor in Sister Bay to plan your trip.

(920) 854 – 7598
www.kayakdoorcounty.com

• 32 •

Dine at a classic Wisconsin Supper Club.

Dining at a true Wisconsin Supper Club is an experience to be cherished, and among dining options, it is a vanishing breed. You will first head into the bar, a warm and inviting haven that has not changed for decades. The bartender will set you up with menus and a couple of drinks. While you are perusing the menu, enjoy the selection of Wisconsin cheeses and crackers. Your server will take your dinner order and then invite you to the table when your salads have been served. One of our favorites is the Mill Supper Club at the junction of Hwy 42/57 on the north side of Sturgeon Bay.

(920) 743 - 5044

• 33 •

Trek to a secret place.

Just north of Ellison Bay on Hwy 42 there is a little sign which reads "NP." This is the easily missed access road that takes you to the front gate of Newport State Park. Drive north to the 3rd parking lot, and then follow the Lynd Point Trail north along the Lake Michigan Shore. One of my favorite little places in all the world is the rocky point on the northern tip of Lynd Point. On a day when the lake is calm, you will feel renewed by the serenity of Europe Bay.

Fish Creek, Clark Park

• 34 •

Indulge at Wilson's Ice Cream Parlor in Ephraim. Often.

• 35 •

Dedicate a day to the arts, stop in every art gallery you see.

Even if you rarely frequent art galleries, take a one-day detour from the ordinary and discover the extraordinary depth of talent gathered in the arts community of Door County. From pottery to woven tapestry to blown glass, you will find world-class artists throughout the county. One of our favorites and a great place to start your day is Edgewood Orchard Galleries, just east of Hwy 42 to the south of Fish Creek on Peninsula Players Road.

(920) 868 – 3579

• 36 •

Escape <u>from</u> Door County?

When you live in Door County, it is hard to imagine going anywhere else for a summer vacation. Here is one of our favorite little escapes from the crowds on the mainland. Spend a weekend at The Washington Hotel on Washington Island and take a course at their culinary school; you will gather your own morels, rhubarb and ramps from the hotel grounds then create a memorable dish from these and other local delights. Classes are offered throughout the year. If you do not stay the night, make sure to have lunch or dinner in the hotel restaurant, where multi-course meals are served using locally grown organic ingredients.

www.thewashingtonhotel.com

(920) 847 – 2169

• 37 •

Do the Hairpin Run on the 4th of July.

Run (or walk) the Hairpin 5k Race in Fish Creek the morning of the 4th of July. The race starts in the bank parking lot at the corner of Hwy 42 and Main Street and finishes behind Founder's Square. This is a great way to start a memorable and active family day; for many it has become a tradition.

• 38 •

Get a taste of local life at the
Door County Fair in August.
The fair grounds are located just
west of Hwy 42 in
Sturgeon Bay.

• 39 •

Dance to live jazz on the pristine waters of Garrett Bay.

Wait for the perfect evening (warm temperatures and calm breezes), then enjoy a little romance on the Sunset Concert Cruise. The cruise sets sail from the Island Clipper dock in Gills Rock. The Captain narrates a short cruise, and then turns off the engines so guests can enjoy dinner and live entertainment while quietly drifting along the picturesque bluffs of northern Door County.

www.concertcruises.com
(920) 854 – 2986

• 40 •

Stop in and say hello to one of Door County's original artisans at the Potter's Wheel, across from Gibraltar High School in Fish Creek.

• 41 •

See a legend of the great lakes: The Edward L. Ryerson iron ore ship.

Head to Sturgeon Bay and follow 3rd Avenue across Michigan Avenue where it turns into Memorial Drive; turn right on Pennsylvania Street and you should see this 1000 footer looming overhead. Sitting high in the water, void of her iron ore load, you can see the gargantuan prop protruding from the water – it's a sight to behold.

• 42 •

Don't miss Door County's Grand Finale.

Plan a special visit to Door County just for Egg Harbor's Pumpkin Patch Festival. This is the king of all Door County Festivals and is not to be missed. Enjoy all day music in Harbor View Park, face painting and rides for the kids, one of the best parades of the year and all your favorite treats of the fall season.

(920) 868 - 3717

• 43 •

*Go ice skating
under the stars at
Sister Bay's outdoor rink.*

• 44 •

Spend an afternoon on Sturgeon Bay's historic 3rd Avenue.

This gathering of shops, restaurants and galleries harkens back to the small town main streets of the 1950's. Start your day at the Door County Historical Museum (920-743-5809) at 18 N. 4th Avenue, and then do the shops of 3rd Avenue. Enjoy lunch at the Inn at Cedar Crossing, and then cross the bridge and spend a couple of hours at the Door County Maritime Museum (920-743-5958.)

• 45 •

Pick up some squeaky cheese curds!

Kick off your visit to the county with a bag of fresh cheese curds from Renard's Cheese Factory, located on both Highways S and 57, south of Sturgeon Bay. Make sure to ask for the curds so fresh they squeak!

Hwy S (920) 743 – 6626
Hwy 57 (920) 825 – 7272

Candlelight Skiing, Peninsula State Park

• 46 •

Ski by candlelight through one of Door County's State Parks.

You must do this at least once in your lifetime. When you have skied deep into the woods, stop and listen. On a cold, calm night, you can almost hear the beat of your own heart. Few ever experience this side of Door County first hand. At the end of the one mile, candle-lit loop you will be welcomed by a rolling bonfire and refreshments at the warming shelter.

(920) 868 – 3258

• 47 •

Tell the Captain you want to pop the chute and bury the rail. Then hold on for the ride of your life!

There is a magical moment that happens every time I go sailing. A feeling of joy and exhilaration sweeps over me during those first few moments after the engine goes silent and the quiet power of the wind takes over. I recommend Sail Door County.

www.saildoorcounty.com

(920) 495-SAIL

• 48 •

Hop in the car, find an orchard with a "pick your own" sign out front (they're everywhere), grab a pail and revel in one of life's simple pleasures – picking your own cherries, apples, strawberries, pumpkins …etc.

• 49 •

Spend a night in one of Sister Bay's historical landmarks.

One of Sister Bay's oldest historical buildings is home to the Inn on Maple, a place where French toast for breakfast means first baking the bread from scratch. This kind of attention to detail gets harder to find every year, and it's why we love this Inn.

(920) 854 – 5107

• 50 •

Cap off your day with a margarita (or two) at JJ's La Puerta in Seester Bay.

One of the local's favorite finishes to a long, hard day of work or play in Door County is a margarita at JJ's on Hwy 42 at the north end of Sister Bay. Keep the made-from-scratch chips and salsa coming! Don't forget to say hello to the two stiffs at the bar. (Check out the barstools on the corner.)

• 51 •

Bake a Door County Cherry Pie

~Pastry for a 2-crust 9" pie.
~6 cups frozen Door County Cherries or (2) 16 oz. cans of water-packed Door County Cherries, drained. You can find either of these at most of Door County's farm stands.
~3 tablespoons tapioca (quick-cooking.)
~1&1/3 cups sugar.
~1/4 teaspoon almond extract.

Combine fruit, tapioca, sugar and extract in bowl; let stand 15 minutes. Fill pastry shell with fruit mixture; dot with one tablespoon butter or margarine. Add top crust; seal and flute edges. Cut slits in top pastry to allow steam to escape. Bake at 400 degrees for 65 -70 minutes. Serve warm with vanilla ice cream.

• 52 •

Hunt for the giant Sturgeon of Sturgeon Bay.

You may have heard of the decorated cows of Chicago, well they had to get the idea from somewhere, and yes, you guessed it – they stole the idea from Sturgeon Bay. Only up here in *da nort*, we decorate giant Sturgeon. The sculptures are unveiled in May and are situated all around town. Take a walking tour of Sturgeon Bay and see how many you can find.

(920) 743 – 6246

• 53 •

Grab your lawn chairs and take in a "Concert in the Park" on Wednesday afternoons at 3:00 pm in the Sister Bay Village Park.

• 54 •

Gather family and friends for a flotilla of fun at Nicolet Bay.

As a local, my family's favorite way to play tourist for a day is on the waters of Eagle Harbor in Ephraim. Treat yourself to a cooler full of specialty foods and beverages, rent one of those silly looking pontoon boats, then cruise over to Nicolet Bay to join the flotilla of yachts. What better way to relax than on your own private island! The sand bay is great for swimming and the beachfront pavilion has all the facilities a family needs.

Fyr Bal Festival, Ephraim

• 55 •

Celebrate the burning of the "winter witch" at the Fyr Bal Festival.

On the summer solstice, head to Ephraim just before sunset to see the "burning of the winter witch." Every year the Scandinavian Fyr Bal Festival welcomes the beginning of summer by setting symbolic bonfires around the perimeter of Eagle Harbor and crowning a Fyr Bal Chieftain. The ceremony is capped by a fireworks display on Saturday evening.

(920) 854 - 4989

• 56 •

Go to a drive-in movie at one of Wisconsin's last great open-air theatres.

Take lots of blankets and pillows and sit under the stars on the lawn up front. Save room for a snack, the concessions offer foot-longs and fresh-baked pizzas! Located just a mile north of Fish Creek on Hwy 42.

• 57 •

Our family's favorite bike route:

For a wonderful afternoon of biking, try this route. Park your car at the Ellison Bay Men's Club Park (at the corner of Garrett Bay and School Road). Hop on your bikes and follow Garrett Bay Road to the north (about 1.5 miles), when you reach a stop sign turn right up the steep hill, at the top of the hill turn left and follow Cottage Road all of the way to Gills Rock (about 1.5 miles). Stop in Charlie's Smoke House for some fresh smoked fish, or have lunch at the Shoreline Restaurant. Then follow Hwy 42 just a block north and turn left on Wisconsin Bay Road. Spend some time at the Door County Maritime Museum and then head back the way you came.

• 58 •

Take the kids on a Playground Parade – spend the entire day hitting the playgrounds in every town in the county. They will remember this day forever.

• 59 •

See a Shakespeare play in the Garden at Bjorklunden.

www.doorshakespear.com

• 60 •

Ask a local where their favorite "spot" is to just sit and soak up the scenery. I guarantee you will be led to a unique and beautiful place every time.

• 61 •

Having a rainy day and don't know what to do?

Head to the Door County institution known as the Sister Bay Bowl. You will all have a blast bowling, and when you are done, stick around for dinner and find out why this is also home to one of the county's most popular dining rooms.

(920) 854 – 2841

• 62 •

Visit Door County's oldest continuously operated grocery store.

Long after the tourist season ends, and the bays are frozen over, there is one store that the locals trust to be open everyday: The Pioneer in Ellison Bay. It is like taking a step back in time; the store is still heated in the winter by an antique potbelly wood stove, and you will most likely have to enlist the owner's help to find all of the items on your list (and we would not want it any other way.)

• 63 •

Go to Schoolhouse Beach on Washington Island at sunset; if you're looking for romance, you'll be swept away.

Take the car ferry across, then follow Lobdell Point Road to Main Street, turn right onto Jackson Harbor Road, then left onto Schoolhouse Beach Road.

Highway 42 between Gills Rock & Northport

• 64 •

Get off the beaten path!

Take a drive by a different set of rules – you can go anywhere you like without using Hwy 42 or 57. Do not be afraid to get lost, remember Door County is just like a big island. You will never be far from finding yourself, and getting lost can lead to some wonderful discoveries. By the end of the day, you will have found your own secret "spot."

• 65 •

If you're an outdoor enthusiast, Rock Island is your paradise found.

Did you know there is a place in Door County where cars and not even bikes are allowed? From 1910-1945 a wealthy inventor owned what is now Rock Island State Park off the northern tip of Washington Island, and this 912-acre park is true paradise. Take the Karfi Ferry from Washington to Rock Island, and do not miss a visit to the Great Hall of the massive stone boathouse.

(920) 847 - 2235

Rock Island, Boat House

• 66 •

Be a gear head for the night; see the stock car races on Saturday nights at the County Fairgrounds in Sturgeon Bay.

• 67 •

See the hard working goats on the roof of Al Johnson's Restaurant.

Go to Al Johnson's restaurant to see the goats on the grass roof of the authentic Swedish building. Take a picture with the goats behind you in the distance so that it appears a tiny goat is standing on your head! (They also make some pretty popular Swedish pancakes.)

• 68 •

Feel the thrill of a snowmobile ride through Peninsula State Park.

Rent a few snowmobiles, bundle up and explore the endless miles of trails throughout the county. You will find some of the best riding in Peninsula State Park. Many businesses rent snowmobiles, but Fish Creek Marine is closest to the park.

(920) 868 - 3909

• 69 •

*Snowshoe the
Peninsula State Park golf course
by the light of the moon.*

• 70 •

Pick up a slice of Americana at one of our favorite farm markets.

When you are in Door County on vacation, you have to shop the farm markets. Our family has a few favorites: Lautenbach's (just south of Fish Creek on Hwy 42), Seaquist's (south of Ellison Bay on Hwy 42), Wood Orchard (north of Egg Harbor on Hwy 42), Koepsel's (south of Sister Bay on Hwy 57), and Schartner's (south of Egg Harbor on Hwy 42.)

• 71 •

*When the moon is full, take
your loved one for a walk
along the beaches of
Whitefish Dunes.*

• 72 •

Strap on your overalls and be a farmer for a day at <u>THE</u> Farm.

Get a taste of life on a real Wisconsin farm at this living, working farm museum. This is a long-time Door County tradition that is a must-see with or without kids. Feed goat kids, witness chicks hatching, and hike the nature trails. <u>THE</u> FARM is always one of the local kids' favorite field trips. Spend a day in the country and find out why. Just north of Sturgeon Bay on Hwy 42.

(920) 743-6666

• 73 •

Find the treasure of Door County's "inner" coast.

The days are few in Door County when the water temperatures rise above "shocking" and enter the "refreshing" zone. You will find warmer water and thinner crowds at our favorite inland lake: Clarks Lake Beach. Follow County WD (Clarks Lake Road) East from Hwy 57 in Jacksonport, then turn left on Park Road and look for the beach area.

• 74 •

Spend a day on the north beach of Chamber's Island.

If you have a boat, (or better- have friends who have a boat) you'll be able to find your way to a hidden treasure just off of Door County's west coast: the crescent shaped beach on the north shore of Chamber's Island. This is the quintessential Door County day-trip by boat. It is a very rustic destination with no public facilities, so travel prepared. (Legend has it that Chambers Island was one of Al Capone's hide-a-ways during his reign as the top Chicago mobster.)

• 75 •

Go on a photo safari for Bald Eagles.

There is no sight more majestic than that of an American Bald Eagle soaring through the skies. If you have experience in bird watching, you may be able to catch a glimpse of one of these elusive giants. Here is how to increase your chances: from Hwy 42 in Sister Bay, follow Hwy ZZ all the way to the dead end. At the Wagon Trail Resort, rent a kayak, pack your binoculars and a camera and head toward Rowley's Bay near the mouth of the Mink River. If you happen to see an Eagle, remember to keep at least several hundreds yards distance and do not approach once it has been sited. Capture the moment with a photograph, and respect the seclusion Eagles need to survive.

Eagle Tower, Peninsula State Park

• 76 •

Tour the Towers.

Plan a day of touring the observation towers of Door County. Start your day in Sturgeon Bay with breakfast at the Bluefront Café on 3rd Avenue, then head to the Potowatomi State Park - follow Shore Road to the tower. Next, head north on Hwy 42 to Fish Creek and stop at Digger's to pick up a picnic lunch; then continue north to the Fish Creek entrance of Peninsula State Park. Enter the park and follow Shore Road to Eagle Tower, Eagle Trail (2.0 miles) and Eagle Panorama, all accessible from a wonderful picnic area where you can enjoy your lunch.

• 77 •

Mini-golf the Little Red Putter located between Sister Bay and Ephraim on Hwy 42 and then have your entire family sit in the giant rocker for a portrait.

• 78 •

Saddle up and hit the trails.

If you hanker for a taste of the old west, you will feel like you are back on the Ponderosa Ranch when you take a ride at Kurtz Corral. Every ride includes a brief lesson to help you brush up your skills, and then, depending on your comfort level, you can ride the arena, the woods or a trail. If you have the chance, go for a ride during the winter the morning after a fresh snow – pure magic.

(920) 743-6742

• 79 •

Kayak over the shipwreck in North Bay.

Here is another kayak adventure: hunt for the shallow-water shipwreck in the waters of North Bay. Follow County Road ZZ out of Sister Bay to North Bay Road go all the way to the dead end. You will be able to put in at the small public launch. Just off the coast, in waters no deeper that 4 feet is a shipwreck clearly visible from the surface. Be sure not to disturb the old timbers so that others can enjoy it for years to come.

• 80 •

Plan your own progressive dinner!

Here is our suggestion for adventures in dining. Start in Gill's Rock at the Shoreline for cocktails over sunset. Next, head south on Hwy 42 to Ellison Bay, turn left on Mink River Road and have a seat in the bar area at T.Ashwell's for hors d' oeuvres (our favorite is the coconut shrimp) and the spirited sounds of live piano. Now continue south on Hwy 42 to Sister Bay and dinner at the Inn at Kristoffer's. To cap the evening, get back on Hwy 42 and drive south to Fish Creek where you will step upstairs to Mr. Helsinki (above the Fish Creek Market) and enjoy a unique menu of desert crepes on a par with the best Parisian creperies.

• 81 •

Learn about the lighthouse life.

Take part in the annual, countywide
Lighthouse Walk each year in mid-May. Start at the
Door county Maritime Museum and take the trolley
to 6 mainland lighthouses for a guided, behind-the-
scenes tour of life at a lighthouse.

www.dcmm.org

Cana Island Lighthouse

• 82 •

Attack the mountain bike trails at Peninsula State Park.

Ride into the main entrance of the park and stay to the right where you will see the Sunset Bike Trail head. Follow this crushed gravel path until you come to the entrance to the mountain bike trails less than ½ mile in on the right hand side. You will find some of Door County's most challenging and exhilarating rides along the eastern edge of the park. If you need to rent, Nor-Dor Sport & Cyclery rents high-quality bikes at the Fish Creek entrance to the park.

• 83 •

Here is the best plan for an evening in Egg Harbor.

Head to Egg Harbor early on a Thursday evening; do the shops and then meet up at Harbor View Park at 5pm where you will enjoy a live, free, open-air concert (July & August). After the performance, watch the spectacular sunset across the waters of Green Bay and then stroll up to Trio for one of the best Italian dinners on the peninsula.

• 84 •

Don't miss the Washington Island Fly-In Fish Boil.

On one spectacular day each year, private plane owners from across the Midwest set their planes down on the grass landing strip in the middle of Washington Island. They gather for the annual Fly-In Fish Boil, it is open to the public and the take-offs and landings are always a sight to see. For annually updated information:

www.washingtonisland.com

Whitefish Dunes State Park

• 85 •

You will feel like you are on the Carolina Coast at Whitefish Dunes State Park.

For a refreshing departure from the craggy bluffs and rocky shores that make up most of Door County's shoreline, spend a day on Wisconsin's highest sand dunes. Follow Hwy 57 to either North Cave Point Drive or County Road WD to Whitefish Dunes State Park. You will feel like you have traveled to a different part of the world as you walk along the spectacular coastline of the white-sand dunes.

• 86 •

Hike the boardwalk at Ridges Sanctuary.

The "ridges" in the Ridges Sanctuary were formed over hundreds of years as Lake Michigan's shoreline has slowly receded to its current level. This entire sanctuary is now home to an entirely native collection of plants and animals. Take a guided tour and get the full story.

www.ridgesanctuary.org

• 87 •

*On a crystal clear night,
go star gazing by canoe
on the calm waters
of Europe Lake.*

• 88 •

See the architectural masterpiece that is home to the Guenzel Gallery.

The round barn that is the Guenzel Gallery at the Peninsula Art School is as much a work of art as the collection inside. The barn is a hidden landmark, surrounded by a sculpture garden and filled with the work of renowned local and national artists. Plan a visit as part of your day in Fish Creek. Follow Hwy 42 to the north edge of town then turn right on County Road F.

• 89 •

Tour one of Door County's largest dairy farms.

One of Door County's newest destinations that we include in the "instant classic" category is the Dairy View Country Store. This working Wisconsin farm is a great place for a family visit - take the tour, watch as the cows are milked, enjoy a fresh, homemade ice cream, and then play tag with the kids in the corn maze. Follow Hwy 42 north to Carlsville, then turn east on County I.

www.dairyview.com
(920) 743-9779

• 90 •

Have cocktails at sunset on the shores of North Bay.

Door County's best places are always a little hard to find, and Gordon Lodge's Top Deck Lounge is at the top of that list. When we need a little escape from the day to day, my wife and I always look forward to sunset cocktails on the shores of secluded North Bay. The Top Deck has not changed much in the last 30 years; some places just cannot be improved. Follow Hwy 57 to County Road Q then turn on Pine Drive to the resort.

• 91 •

The best way to get wet on a rainy day.

Having a rainy day and don't know what to do with the family? Head to the YMCA in Fish Creek or Sturgeon Bay. Play a little basketball, use the weight room, and then go for a swim. The Sturgeon Bay pool even has indoor water slides and a toddler area. This rainy day might turn out to be one of the most memorable of the trip.

www.doorcountyymca.org

• 92 •

Take a little "me" time and be pampered at the spa.

Where do the locals go for a little pampering? The Spa at Sacred Grounds. Even if you are here for a family vacation, take a few hours for yourself and schedule a little "me" time. Unwind in the sauna or steam bath, and then have the tension massaged away. Located just off Hwy 42 between Ephraim and Sister Bay on Townline Road.

(920) 854-4733

Sawyer Harbor, Sturgeon Bay

• 93 •

*Go off the grid for a day.
No radio, no TV, no car,
just you and the calming,
rejuvenating affect of Door
County's natural beauty – get
outside and play!*

• 94 •

See what Door County was like before 2 million people came to visit.

Many visitors to Door County talk about the way things "used" to be. Get a taste of what the county was like years ago: head to Ellison Bay for the day. This sleepy little town just 3 miles north of Sister Bay is home to The Viking - Door County's original fish boil; The Pioneer - the county's oldest continuously operated general store, The Silly Goose - one of the county's original gift shops, established in 1968, and many other shops, restaurants and hotels. (I may be a little biased here - it is also my family's adopted hometown, and we love every quirk and character in it.)

• 95 •

The best gifts are made by hand.

Here is another great rainy day (or sunny day) activity whether you are with the family, a group of friends or just a couple: Hands On Art Studio. Door County is full of art studios, so get inspired and create a little art of your own. Located in a 1960's round-roofed barn, the rustic surroundings will give you room to breath and express your creativity. Can you still conjure that finger-painting feeling of joy you had as a child? This is the place to find your inner artist again. Located on Peninsula Players Road just east of Hwy 42, (920) 868-9311.

www.handsonartstudio.com

• 96 •

Teach the kids to golf.

Do you love to golf, and would like to be able to teach the kids, but worry about the course frowning on the presence of children? Stonehedge Golf Course loves kids, encourages getting them involved early and best of all, is one of Door County's most affordable courses. Take a day and teach the kids to golf at Stonehedge – it is the perfect place for them to get started. Located just east of Hwy 42 in Egg Harbor on County Road E.

(920) 868 - 2566

• 97 •

Renew your vows at Stavkirke in the woods.

Prove to your loved one that your bond is still strong and true. Take the car ferry over to Washington Island and then follow Lobdell Point Road to Main Street, turn left on Main, then right on Townline Road. Pull over and hike the short trail to Stavkirke, a magical replica of the Stave Church in Norway surrounded by woods. Take her to the center of the little chapel and tell her you would do it all again.

• 98 •

See the spectacle of shipbuilding at Bay Ship.

Start with lunch at Perry's Cherry Diner on Michigan Avenue in Sturgeon Bay, and then walk toward the shipyards at the end of 3rd Avenue. When you reach the end of the main shopping district, keep going. Follow 3rd Avenue for another 2 blocks where you will see the spectacular work of Bay Ship Building. If you are lucky, you will get to see one of the great lakes 1000 footers in dry dock. Getting close to these giant ships is always a humbling experience.

• 99 •

Skip a few rocks at Pebble Beach.

Take Hwy 42 to East Little Sister Road at the base of the big hill, turn right and then follow Pebble Beach Road at the fork. You will dead end at Pebble Beach. This is also a spectacular spot to observe the northern lights when they are visible. After your visit to the beach, grab lunch at one of Door County's best-kept secrets: Fred & Fuzzy's. This outdoor, waterfront restaurant is one of our favorites. On your way back to Hwy 42, turn left onto W. Little Sister Road and park along the stone wall. The restaurant is just 50 yards down the hill toward the water.

The Barn at Anderson Dock, Ephraim

• 100 •

Make a splash at the Classic and Wooden Boat Show.

Do not miss the annual classic and wooden boat show held each summer in Sturgeon Bay at the Door County Maritime Museum. Marvel at these gorgeous hand-made works of art, enjoy the sailing, diving and kayaking demonstrations, and then get involved in the family activities.

www.dcmm.org

• 101 •

Discover one of southern Door County's natural jewels: the Ahnapee State Trail / Ice Age National Scenic Trail.

Load up the bikes and head to Forestville on Hwy 42, where you can bike a section of the trail that borders the Forestville Flowage. If you are feeling adventurous you can ride the trail all of the way from Sturgeon Bay to Algoma.

• 102 •

Find your thrills on Hill 17.

Door County die-hards know winter can be the best time of all to come for a visit; and one of our favorite days starts with a giant inner tube rental at Nor-Dor Sport & Cyclery in Fish Creek. Tie down your new toy and head to Hill 17 in Peninsula State Park. If you crave adrenaline, I guarantee you will not be disappointed – this hill rivals tube runs in the Rockies. Put a helmet on the little ones, stay alert (and out of the woods), and have a blast!

· 103 ·

The best thing to do is simply spend time with family and friends.

Now that you have reached the end, I will assume you have completed every item on the list! Maybe this is a good time to remind you that even with all of the wonderful things to do in Door County, the best thing you will find up here … is time. Time to remove yourself from the distractions of life – no work, no school, no worries, and spend a few days focused on the simple gift of each other.

Dear Rich,

Here is an idea our family hopes you will include in the next edition ….

I would love to hear all of your great ideas! Please share your secret with me at:

The Rusnack Family
P.O. Box 347
Ellison Bay, WI 54210
rrusnack@dcwis.com

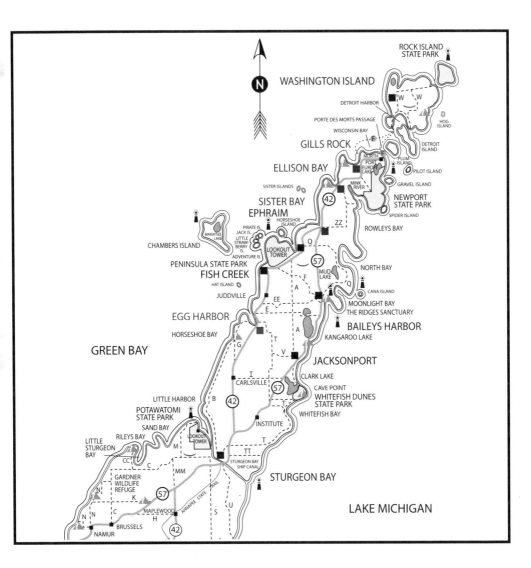

To order
101 Things To do In Door County:

email:	rrusnack@dcwis.com
fax:	920.854.6612
phone:	414.405.5335
snail mail:	Rusnack Publishing
	P.O. Box 347
	Ellison Bay, WI 54210

RusnackPublishing